The Wheels on the Bus

To Alice Kovalski

Maryann Kovalski

The Wheels on the Bus

HOUGHTON MIFFLIN COMPANY
BOSTON
ATLANTA DALLAS GENEVA, ILLINOIS PALO ALTO PRINCETON

One day, Grandma took Jenny and Joanna
shopping for new winter coats.

They tried on long coats and short coats,
blue coats and red coats, plaid coats and even
raincoats. Joanna chose a coat with wooden
barrel buttons. Jenny liked it too,
because of the hood.

When it was time to go home, the bus didn't come for a long time and everyone grew tired. "I have an idea, sweeties," said Grandma. "Let's sing a song my Granny sang with me when I was a little girl." And so they began to sing. . . .

The wheels on the bus go round and round round and round round and round. The wheels on the bus go round and round all around the town.

The wipers on the bus go swish, swish, swish

swish, swish, swish

swish, swish, swish

The wipers on the bus go swish, swish, swish

all around the town.

The people on the bus hop on and off

on and off

on and off

The people on the bus hop on and off

all around the town.

The horn on the bus goes toot, toot, toot

   toot, toot, toot

   toot, toot, toot

The horn on the bus goes toot, toot, toot

   all around the town.

The money on the bus goes clink, clink, clink

   clink, clink, clink

   clink, clink, clink

The money on the bus goes clink, clink, clink

   all around the town.

The people on the bus go up and down

up and down

up and down

The people on the bus go up and down

all around the town.

The babies on the bus go waaa, waaa, waaa

waaa, waaa, waaa

waaa, waaa, waaa

The babies on the bus go waaa, waaa, waaa

all around the town.

The parents on the bus go ssh, ssh, ssh

    ssh, ssh, ssh

    ssh, ssh, ssh

The parents on the bus go ssh, ssh, ssh

    all around the town.

The wheels on the bus go round and round

round and round

round and round

The wheels on the bus go round and round

all around the town.

Grandma, Jenny, and Joanna had so much fun . . .

They missed the bus!

So . . .

They took a taxi.